Pebble® Plus

Dinosaurs and Prehistoric Animals
Giganotosaurus

by Janet Riehecky

Consulting Editor: Gail Saunders-Smith, PhD

Consultant: Jack Horner, Curator of Paleontology
Museum of the Rockies
Bozeman, Montana

Capstone press®

Mankato, Minnesota

Pebble Plus is published by Capstone Press,
151 Good Counsel Drive, P.O. Box 669, Mankato, Minnesota 56002.
www.capstonepress.com

1 2 3 4 5 6 14 13 12 11 10 09

Library of Congress Cataloging-in-Publication Data
Riehecky, Janet, 1953–
    Giganotosaurus / by Janet Riehecky.
    p. cm. — (Pebble Plus. Dinosaurs and prehistoric animals)
    Summary: "Simple text and illustrations present prehistoric giganotosaurus, how it looked, and what
it did" — Provided by publisher.
    Includes bibliographical references and index.
    ISBN-13: 978-1-4296-0038-5 (hardcover)
    ISBN-10: 1-4296-0038-1 (hardcover)
    1. Giganotosaurus — Juvenile literature. I. Title. II. Series.
QE862.S3R5357 2007
567.912 — dc22   2006102255

Editorial Credits
Sarah L. Schuette and Jenny Marks, editors; Gene Bentdahl, designer; Wanda Winch, photo researcher

Illustration and Photo Credits
Jon Hughes, illustrator
Courtesy of Kris Kripchak, 21

Note to Parents and Teachers

The Dinosaurs and Prehistoric Animals set supports national science standards related to
the evolution of life. This book describes and illustrates giganotosaurus. The images support
early readers in understanding the text. The repetition of words and phrases helps early readers
learn new words. This book also introduces early readers to subject-specific vocabulary words,
which are defined in the Glossary section. Early readers may need assistance to read some
words and to use the Table of Contents, Glossary, Read More, Internet Sites, and Index sections
of the book.

Table of Contents

giganotosaurus (jig-a-NOTE-uh-SORE-us)

A Big Meat Eater

Giganotosaurus was

one of the longest dinosaurs

that ate meat.

It walked

on two clawed feet.

Giganotosaurus lived
in prehistoric times.
It lived in South America
100 million years ago.

How Giganotosaurus Looked

Giganotosaurus was about
47 feet (14 meters) long.
It was as long
as a big bus.

Giganotosaurus had
a thin, pointy tail.
It held its tail straight out
as it walked.

Giganotosaurus had
two small hands.
Each hand had three fingers
with sharp claws.

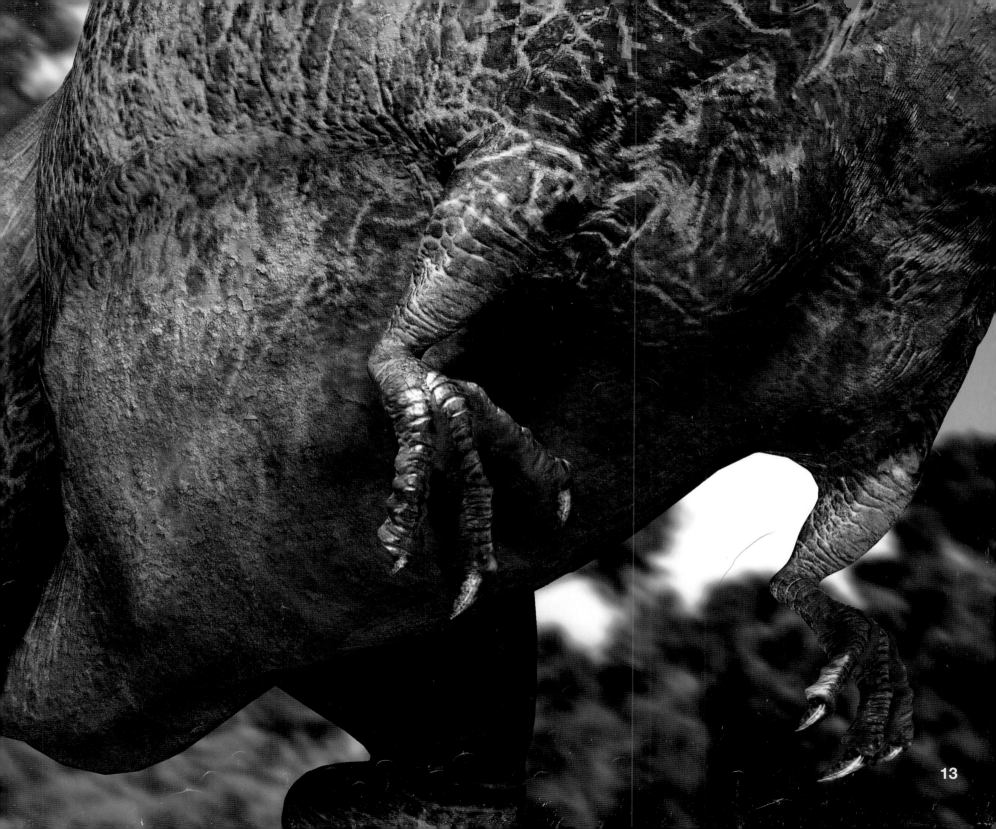

What Giganotosaurus Did

Giganotosaurus had
a good sense of smell.
It could smell prey far away.

Giganotosaurus attacked
large plant eaters.

It may have hunted in packs.

Giganotosaurus chewed
with very sharp teeth.
Its teeth were shaped
like arrow tips.

The End of Giganotosaurus

Giganotosaurus died out

millions of years ago.

No one knows why.

Today, you can see

their fossils in museums.

Glossary

claw — a long, curved nail on an animal's foot or hand

fossil — the remains or traces of an animal or a plant, preserved as rock

museum — a place where objects of art, history, or science are shown

pack — a small group of animals that hunts together

prehistoric — very old; prehistoric means belonging to a time before history was written down.

prey — an animal that is hunted for food

Read More

Christiansen, Per. *Prehistoric Beasts.* Nature's Monsters. Pleasantville, New York: Gareth Stevens, 2009.

Lunis, Natalie. *Savage Slashers.* Dino Times Triva. New York: Bearport, 2009.

Matthews, Rupert. *Dinosaurs in Action.* Dinosaur Dig. Mankato, Min.: QEB Publishing, 2009.

Internet Sites

FactHound offers a safe, fun way to find educator-approved Internet sites related to this book.

Here's what you do:

1. Visit www.facthound.com
2. Choose your grade level.
3. Begin your search.

This book's ID number is 9781429600385.

FactHound will fetch the best sites for you!

Index

Word Count: 130
Grade: 1
Early-Intervention Level: 16